COMPARING ANIMAL TRAITS

SIBERIAN TIGERS

CAMOUFLAGED HUNTING MAMMALS

REBECCA E. HIRSCH

Lerner Publications ◆ Minneapolis

Lerner Publications Company
A division of Lerner Publishing Group, Inc.
241 First Avenue North
Minneapolis, MN 55401 USA

For reading levels and more information, look up this title at www.lernerbooks.com.

Photo Acknowledgments

The images in this book are used with the permission of: © John Hyde/Perspectives/Getty Images, p. 1; © blickwinkel/Alamy, p. 4; © Levi Tomes, pp. 5, 9 (left); © Horizon International Images Limited/Alamy, p. 6; © iStockphoto.com/Byrdyak, p. 7 (top); © davemhuntphotography/iStock/Thinkstock, p. 7 (bottom); © iStockphoto.com/EcoPic, p. 8; © iStockphoto.com/WLDavies, p. 9 (right); © Frans Lanting/Mint IImages/ Getty Images, p. 10; © Steve P/Alamy, p. 11 (top left); © Roland Seitre/Getty Images, p. 11 (top right); © Laura Westlund/Independent Picture Service, p. 12; © iStockphoto.com/ProjectB, p. 13 (top); © Natphotos/ Digital Vision/Getty Images, p. 13 (bottom); © JillLang/iStock/Thinkstock, p. 14; © Arterra Picture Library/ Alamy, p. 15 (top left); © johnrandallalves/iStock/Thinkstock, p. 15 (top right); © Jupiterimages/Photos. com/Thinkstock, p. 15 (bottom left); © David Tipling/Lonely Planet Images/Getty Images, p. 16; © Krys Bailey/Alamy, p. 17 (Left); © Vario Images GmbH & Co.KG/Alamy, p. 17 (right); © Design Pics Inc./Alamy, p. 18; © Anna Henly/Getty Images, p. 19 (top); © TAO Images Limited/Alamy, p. 19 (bottom); © Wayne Lynch/ All Canada Photos/Getty Images, p. 20; © Tierfotoagentur /Alamy, p. 21 (left); © All Canada Photos/Alamy, pp. 21 (right), 27 (bottom left); © Cyrille Gibot/Alamy, p. 22; © iStockphoto.com/mb-photos, p. 23 (top); © Dave J Williams/Alamy, p. 23 (bottom); © iStockphoto.com/photos_marYmage, p. 24; © iStockphoto.com/ MiStock, p. 25 (top); © Xinhua/Alamy, pp. 25 (bottom), 29 (left); © LOOK Die Bildagentur der Fotografen GmbH/Alamy, p. 26; © Eric Gevaert/Hemera/Thinkstock, p. 27 (top left); © Geoff Kuchera/iStock/ Thinkstock, p. 27 (top right); © iStockphoto.com/CraigRJD, p. 28; © Dave Watts/naturepl.com, p. 29 (right).

Front cover: © Tim Fitzharris/Minden Pictures/Getty Images.
Back cover: © iStockphoto.com/aznature.

Main body text set in Calvert MT Std 12/18. Typeface provided by Monotype Typography.

Library of Congress Cataloging-in-Publication Data

Hirsch, Rebecca E., author.
    Siberian tigers : camouflaged hunting mammals / by Rebecca E. Hirsch.
        pages   cm. — (Comparing animal traits)
    Summary: "This book covers information (life cycle, appearance, habitat) about the Siberian tiger. Each chapter discusses an aspect of the Siberian tiger's life, comparing the tiger to a similar mammal and to a very different mammal."—Provided by publisher.
    Includes index.
    ISBN 978-1-4677-5878-9 (lib. bdg. : alk. paper)
    ISBN 978-1-4677-6065-2 (pbk.)
    ISBN 978-1-4677-6221-2 (EB pdf)
    1. Siberian tiger—Juvenile literature. I. Title.
QL737.C23H565 2015
599.756—dc23   2014028882

Manufactured in the United States of America
1 — BP —12/31/14

TABLE OF CONTENTS

MEET THE SIBERIAN TIGER

A female Siberian tiger and her cubs rest in the forest. As the mother sleeps, her cubs leap and chase one another. The cubs are practicing for when they become fully grown hunters. Siberian tigers belong to a group of animals called mammals. Other groups of animals include insects, fish, amphibians, reptiles, and birds.

Siberian tiger cubs practice their hunting skills by roughhousing with one another.

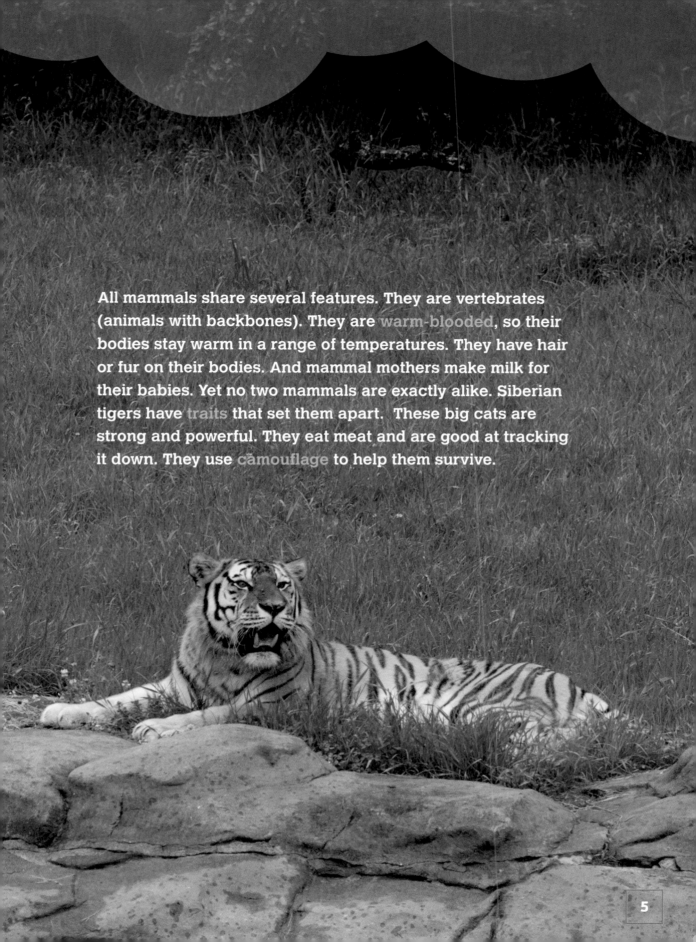

All mammals share several features. They are vertebrates (animals with backbones). They are warm-blooded, so their bodies stay warm in a range of temperatures. They have hair or fur on their bodies. And mammal mothers make milk for their babies. Yet no two mammals are exactly alike. Siberian tigers have traits that set them apart. These big cats are strong and powerful. They eat meat and are good at tracking it down. They use camouflage to help them survive.

CHAPTER 1

WHAT DO SIBERIAN TIGERS LOOK LIKE?

Siberian tigers are the largest cats in the world. Other members of the cat family include African lions, cheetahs, and domestic cats. A male Siberian tiger can reach 12.8 feet (3.9 meters) in length and weigh 660 pounds (300 kilograms). Females are smaller than males.

A Siberian tiger's powerful limbs help it move quickly in the snow.

DID YOU KNOW?
Siberian tigers
are also known as
AMUR TIGERS.
Other types of tigers
include Bengal tigers,
Indochinese tigers, and
Sumatran tigers.

Striped fur covers the Siberian tiger's body. The fur is reddish orange on most of the body. It is creamy white on the belly, the chest, and a few other places. The thick fur keeps the Siberian tiger warm, and the stripes help camouflage the tiger in the forest. The pattern of stripes differs for every tiger. The stripes even differ on each side of the tiger's body.

Siberian tigers are built for hunting. Their large, furry feet help them stalk prey quietly. Their sharp teeth and long claws help them catch and kill prey. The powerful tiger can take down large animals such as deer, elk, and wild boar.

A Siberian tiger steps softly as it stalks its prey.

SIBERIAN TIGERS VS. LEOPARDS

Leopards prowl through grasslands and forests across Africa and Asia. Leopards are medium-sized members of the cat family. Siberian tigers and leopards look similar, but leopards have smaller bodies. From head to tail, a large leopard can reach 10.8 feet (3.3 m). This is not as long as a Siberian tiger.

Siberian tigers and leopards both have round ears, long tails, and thick fur. Flower-shaped spots called rosettes mark a leopard's fur. Like the stripes of a tiger, rosettes camouflage the leopard. When a spotted leopard stands still in a forest or a grassland, the animal's body seems to disappear.

COMPARE IT!

SIBERIAN TIGERS VS. **LEOPARDS**

SIBERIAN TIGERS		LEOPARDS
UP TO 660 POUNDS (300 kg)	◀ WEIGHT ▶	**UP TO 176 POUNDS** (80 kg)
STRIPED	◀ FUR ▶	**SPOTTED**
Sharp and pointy for eating meat	◀ TEETH ▶	Sharp and pointy for eating meat

Both Siberian tigers and leopards have bodies made for hunting. The leopard uses its powerful body, sharp claws, and sharp teeth to catch prey such as antelope. The leopard's slender shape also helps it climb trees. The limbs and the jaws of the leopard are so strong that a leopard sometimes drags its food into a tree before eating the meal.

SIBERIAN TIGERS VS. PANGOLINS

Pangolins forage for insects across Asia and Africa. Pangolins are often called scaly anteaters. They vary in weight from 3.5 pounds (1.6 kg) to 73 pounds (33 kg). Their bodies are much lighter than those of Siberian tigers. Pangolins look different from Siberian tigers too.

Fur covers the bodies of Siberian tigers. But pangolins have hair only on their bellies. Large scales cover the rest of their bodies. These scales make pangolins look like walking pinecones. They also protect the animal from leopards, hyenas, and other predators. The scales are made of the same material as your hair and fingernails. When threatened, the pangolin curls into a scaly ball.

A pangolin uses its claws to dig for insects.

Siberian tigers (*left*) are covered in fur, whereas pangolins (*right*) are covered in scales.

Siberian tigers have sharp teeth. That is not true of pangolins. They don't have any teeth at all. Pangolins use their claws to dig into anthills or termite mounds. Then pangolins slurp up the tasty insects with their long, sticky tongues.

DID YOU KNOW?

Pangolins use their scaly tails to wrap around branches and hang UPSIDE DOWN.

CHAPTER 2

WHERE DO SIBERIAN TIGERS LIVE?

Siberian tigers cross snowy forests in Siberia, a remote part of Russia. A few Siberian tigers also live in China and possibly in North Korea. The forests in these places are thick with birch, oak, and conifer trees. During the long, snowy winters, temperatures can drop to −31°F (−35°C).

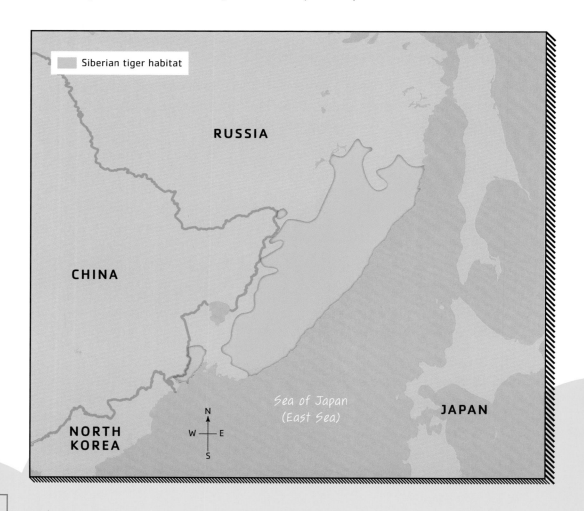

Siberian tiger habitat

RUSSIA

CHINA

NORTH KOREA

Sea of Japan (East Sea)

JAPAN

N
W — E
S

DID YOU KNOW?
In modern times, fewer than **500** Siberian tigers exist in the wild. This makes them an endangered species.

Siberian tigers roam their habitat in search of prey. To keep hidden, they travel through thick brush along paths and roads. Bushes, trees, and fallen logs help tigers stay out of sight. Striped fur helps too. The tigers' bodies blend in perfectly with the trees and the bushes. Tigers also like to stay near water. They need to drink often. On cold days, they take shelter under boulders or logs.

Siberian tigers travel far within their habitat. The tigers cover vast areas to find enough food. Each tiger inhabits a large territory. It defends its territory from other tigers. A Siberian tiger marks the borders of its territory with a scent. It will spray urine or rub its body against trees and bushes.

A Siberian tiger spreads its scent in order to mark its territory.

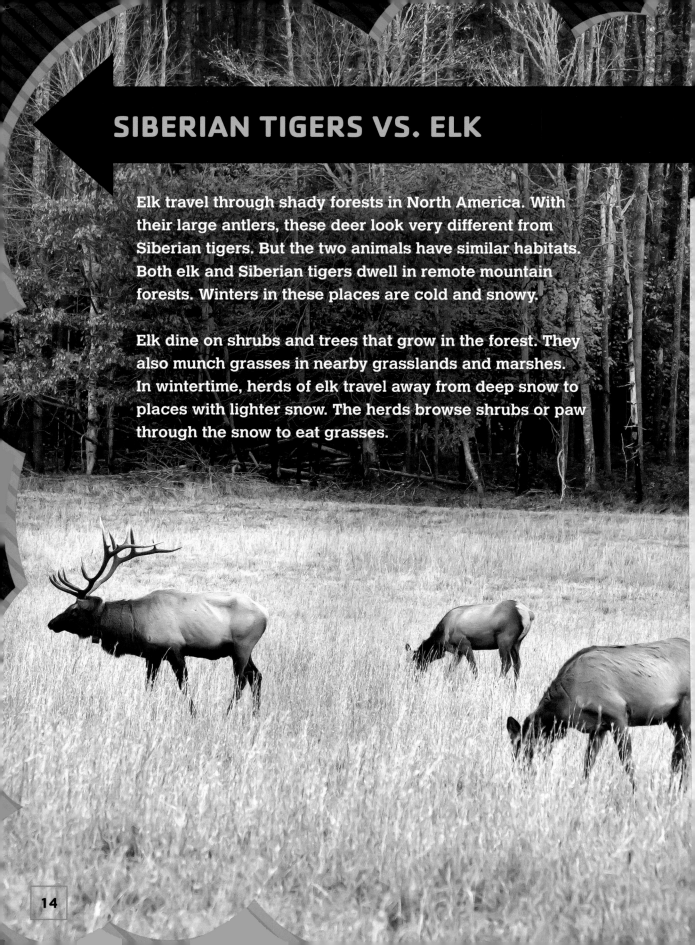

SIBERIAN TIGERS VS. ELK

Elk travel through shady forests in North America. With their large antlers, these deer look very different from Siberian tigers. But the two animals have similar habitats. Both elk and Siberian tigers dwell in remote mountain forests. Winters in these places are cold and snowy.

Elk dine on shrubs and trees that grow in the forest. They also munch grasses in nearby grasslands and marshes. In wintertime, herds of elk travel away from deep snow to places with lighter snow. The herds browse shrubs or paw through the snow to eat grasses.

The fur of both Siberian tigers (*left*) and elk (*right*) provides camouflage.

Both elk and Siberian tigers like to stay unseen within their habitats. Siberian tigers hide so they can stalk prey. Elk hide because they are prey animals. Elk stay out of sight from predators such as gray wolves and grizzly bears. Both elk and Siberian tigers rely on thick brush and trees to avoid being seen by other animals.

DID YOU KNOW?
A male elk's antlers can stand **4 FEET** (1.2 m) tall and weigh up to 40 pounds (18 kg). Females do not have antlers.

15

SIBERIAN TIGERS VS. BACTRIAN CAMELS

Bactrian camels graze on short grasses across the rocky desert in China and Mongolia. Bactrian camels have shaggy coats, long legs, and two humps on their backs. These mammals look quite different from Siberian tigers. They live in different habitats too.

Siberian tigers inhabit cold and snowy forests. Bactrian camels are adapted to survive in the deserts of China and Mongolia. During the summer, temperatures in these deserts can reach 100°F (38°C). Winter temperatures can fall to −20°F (−29°C). Bactrian camels grow a shaggy coat to keep warm in winter. They shed the coat in summer.

Siberian tigers like to stay near water. They finish every meal with a big drink. That's not the case with Bactrian camels. Almost no rain falls in the desert. Water can be hard to find. Bactrian camels rely on fat stored in their humps. Inside a camel's body, fat becomes water and energy. The camel can go more than a week without drinking. When a thirsty camel finds more water, it can gulp down 30 gallons (114 liters) in one session.

COMPARE IT!

SIBERIAN TIGERS

VS.

BACTRIAN CAMELS

NORTHERN FORESTS	◄ HABITAT ►	**DESERT**
RUSSIA, CHINA, POSSIBLY NORTH KOREA	◄ GEOGRAPHIC RANGE ►	**MONGOLIA, CHINA**

Elk, boar, red deer	◄ MAIN FOOD ►	Grasses

CHAPTER 3

HUNTING WITH SIBERIAN TIGERS

Siberian tigers are nocturnal. This means they move about at night. The tigers wait for darkness to fall. Then they stalk through the forest in search of elk, deer, wild boars, and other large prey.

A Siberian tiger hunts alone. It prowls through thick bushes and trees looking and listening for prey. Its feet avoid dry leaves, helping the animal move silently. Its striped coat helps the tiger fade into the surroundings.

A camouflaged Siberian tiger stalks its prey.

Siberian tigers pounce once they reach their prey (*above*). Then they drag their captured prey away to feast on it (*below*).

Once a Siberian tiger spots its prey, it creeps closer and closer. Sometimes it freezes like a statue before moving forward. Finally, it pounces. The tiger often kills its prey with a bite to the throat or the neck.

The powerful predator drags its kill to a hiding place in the brush. The Siberian tiger finishes its meal with a large drink of water. After eating its fill, the tiger covers the carcass with leaves and dirt. It will come back to eat more later.

SIBERIAN TIGERS VS. LONG-TAILED WEASELS

Long-tailed weasels bound through woodlands, thickets, and fields. These slender mammals live in North America and South America. Long-tailed weasels and Siberian tigers inhabit different places. But both animals are carnivores, and they hunt in similar ways.

Both Siberian tigers and long-tailed weasels like to hunt alone. A long-tailed weasel searches for small animals in mice dens, mole burrows, and rabbit holes. It locates prey by scent and sound. Then it stalks an animal and springs with a quick attack. Like Siberian tigers, long-tailed weasels often store extra food for a later meal.

Both Siberian tigers and long-tailed weasels rely on their fur to stay hidden. In northern habitats, long-tailed weasels have cinnamon-brown coats in summer. These coats turn white in winter to blend in with the snow. In warmer places, long-tailed weasels keep their brown coats year-round.

A long-tailed weasel uses its slender body to fit in the hiding spots of prey such as moles and mice.

COMPARE IT!

SIBERIAN TIGERS

VS.

LONG-TAILED WEASELS

THICK FORESTS ◄ WHERE THEY HUNT ► **THICKETS, FIELDS, SMALL WOODLANDS**

STEALTH ◄ HUNTING STRATEGIES ► **STEALTH**

Striped fur ◄ CAMOUFLAGE ► Brown fur in summer, white fur in winter

SIBERIAN TIGERS VS. RING-TAILED LEMURS

Ring-tailed lemurs leap through trees on the African island of Madagascar. These medium-sized mammals have long, striped, black-and-white tails. Siberian tigers hunt by themselves, but ring-tailed lemurs search for food in families. A family contains six to thirty ring-tailed lemurs.

Siberian tigers use their stripes to hide. But stripes serve a very different purpose for ring-tailed lemurs. These animals wave their striped tails like flags. The black-and-white rings make it easy for lemurs to find one another in the forest. That way the family can stay together.

The striped tail of a ring-tailed lemur helps the animal stand out.

Ring-tailed lemurs spend more time in groups than Siberian tigers.

Tigers hunt at night, but lemurs spend their mornings searching for food. The members of a lemur family wake before dawn and then look for fruit, leaves, flowers, and bark. At midday, the lemurs nap on tree branches. The family dines again at nighttime.

DID YOU KNOW?

Male ring-tailed lemurs **"STINK FIGHT"** over territory. They cover their tails with foul smells from their wrists and shoulders. Then they flick their tails at one another.

CHAPTER 4

THE LIFE CYCLE OF SIBERIAN TIGERS

Every stealthy, powerful Siberian tiger begins life as a tiny cub. Female Siberian tigers give birth to between one and five cubs at a time. The newborns cannot move or hear well, and their eyes are closed at birth. Their mother feeds them milk and protects her cubs from predators.

After three months, the cubs are trailing their mother through the forest. They learn to hunt by imitating her. For practice, they pounce on blades of grass or their mother's tail. Sometimes the cubs catch small animals, but they will not begin to hunt large prey until they are at least twelve months old.

A Siberian tiger mother cleans her cub.

A Siberian tiger cub wrestles with its mother.

By eighteen months, the young Siberian tigers are able to hunt alone. They soon leave to find territories of their own. They have inherited traits from their parents, such as sharp teeth and powerful bodies. With these traits, Siberian tigers survive in remote mountain forests for ten to fifteen years.

DID YOU KNOW?
Newborn Siberian tigers weigh no more than **3.5 POUNDS** (1.6 kg). Life for a young tiger is dangerous. Only about half of the cubs in a litter will survive their first year.

SIBERIAN TIGERS VS. BLACK BEARS

Black bears inhabit forests across North America. Like Siberian tigers, black bears are solitary animals. Black bears and Siberian tigers also have similar life cycles. And they raise their young in similar ways.

Female black bears give birth in a winter den. The infant bear cubs cannot see or hear. They also cannot move well. They drink their mother's milk and huddle with her to stay warm. Black bear cubs grow quickly. They are ready to leave the den with their mothers when they are three months old. This is the same age at which Siberian tiger cubs begin to hunt with their mothers.

Black bear cubs stay close to their mother for their first years of life.

Siberian tiger cubs and black bear cubs both depend on their families for safety.

The cubs of both black bears and Siberian tigers usually stay with their mothers for about eighteen months. In some places, black bear cubs stay with their mothers longer, until they are between two and three years old. Black bears usually live longer than Siberian tigers. Siberian tigers live up to fifteen years, but black bears can live about twenty years.

DID YOU KNOW?
Black bear cubs love to romp in the water and **WRESTLE.** Playing helps the cubs prepare to live on their own.

27

SIBERIAN TIGERS VS. TASMANIAN DEVILS

The cries of Tasmanian devils echo through the Australian island of Tasmania. At night, these mammals emerge from logs or burrows to find food. Like Siberian tigers, Tasmanian devils are nocturnal hunters. But Tasmanian devils and Siberian tigers have different life cycles.

Tasmanian devils are marsupials, mammals with pouches. Females give birth to tiny, undeveloped babies called imps.

Tasmanian devils are known for their scream.

About twenty to thirty imps are born at one time. The imps race to survive. They crawl about 3 inches (7.6 centimeters) to their mother's pouch. The first few to arrive attach themselves to the mother's four nipples. Only these four imps will survive.

Tasmanian devils grow up fast. By nine months, they are ready to live on their own. At this age, Siberian tigers still depend on their mothers to feed and protect them. Tasmanian devils live about five or six years, a shorter life span than that of the Siberian tiger.

COMPARE IT!

SIBERIAN TIGERS

VS.

TASMANIAN DEVILS

1 TO 6 PUPS ◀ LITTER SIZE ▶ **20 TO 30 IMPS**

18 MONTHS ◀ AGE OF INDEPENDENT HUNTING ▶ **9 MONTHS**

10 TO 15 YEARS ◀ LIFE SPAN IN THE WILD ▶ **5 TO 6 YEARS**

SIBERIAN TIGER TRAIT CHART

This book explored the ways Siberian tigers are similar to and different from other mammals. What other mammals would you like to learn about?

	WARM-BLOODED	HAIR ON BODY	GIVES BIRTH TO LIVE YOUNG	STRIPED FUR	LIVE IN SNOWY HABITATS	ACTIVE MOSTLY AT NIGHT
SIBERIAN TIGER	X	X	X	X	X	X
LEOPARD	X	X	X		X	X
PANGOLIN	X	X	X			X
ELK	X	X	X		X	
BACTRIAN CAMEL	X	X	X			
LONG-TAILED WEASEL	X	X	X		X	X
RING-TAILED LEMUR	X	X	X	X		
BLACK BEAR	X	X	X		X	
TASMANIAN DEVIL	X	X	X		X	X

GLOSSARY

adapted: suited to living in a particular environment

camouflage: patterns or colors on an animal's body that help the animal blend in with its surroundings

carnivores: meat-eating animals

conifer: evergreen trees and shrubs with needlelike leaves

endangered: at risk of extinction

forage: to search an area for food

habitat: an environment where an animal naturally lives. A habitat is the place where an animal can find food, water, air, shelter, and a place to raise its young.

imitating: following a pattern, a model, or an example

marsupials: mammals whose females have pouches in which they carry their young

nocturnal: active at night

predators: animals that hunt, or prey on, other animals

prey: an animal that a predator hunts and kills for food

solitary: living by itself. Solitary animals spend most of their time alone, except for mating and raising young.

territory: an area that is occupied and defended by an animal or group of animals

traits: features that are inherited from parents. Body size and fur color are examples of traits.

warm-blooded: able to maintain a constant body temperature that is usually warmer than the surrounding environment

LERNER
SOURCE

Expand learning beyond the printed book. Download free, complementary educational resources for this book from our website, www.lerneresource.com.

SELECTED BIBLIOGRAPHY

"The Amur Tiger: Ecology." Wildlife Conservation Society. July 20, 2014. http://www.wcsrussia.org/en-us/wildlife/amurtigers/ecology.aspx.

Karanth, K. Ullas. *The Way of the Tiger*. Stillwater, MN: Voyageur, 2001.

Larson, Jean. "Information Resources on Tigers, Panthera Tigris: Natural History, Ecology, Conservation, Biology, and Captive Care." USDA. July 20, 2014. http://www.nal.usda.gov/awic/pubs/tigers.htm.

Seidensticker, John, and Susan Lumpkin. *Cats: Smithsonian Answer Book*. Washington, DC: Smithsonian Books, 2004.

"Siberian Tiger: *Panthera tigris altaica*." *National Geographic*. March 24, 2014. http://animals.nationalgeographic.com/animals/mammals/siberian-tiger/.

Sunquist, Mel, and Fiona Sunquist. *Wild Cats of the World*. Chicago: University of Chicago Press, 2002.

FURTHER INFORMATION

Biomes of the World—the Taiga
http://www.thewildclassroom.com/biomes/taiga.html
Discover more about the unique forest habitat of the Siberian tiger, known as the taiga.

Carney, Elizabeth. *National Geographic Kids Everything Big Cats*. Washington, DC: National Geographic, 2011. Learn all about tigers, lions, leopards, and jaguars, and compare them to one another.

Johnson, Jinny. *Animal Planet™ Wild World: An Encyclopedia of Animals*. Minneapolis: Millbrook Press, 2012. Pick up this Animal Planet™ encyclopedia to learn more about tigers and many of the world's other fascinating animals.

National Geographic—Siberian Tiger
http://video.nationalgeographic.com/video/tiger_siberian
Watch this video from National Geographic to see how Siberian tigers survive the harsh cold of their habitat.

Panthera—Tigers
http://www.panthera.org/species/tiger
Check out this site from the conservation group Panthera to learn more about all the tigers of the world and the threats they face. The site features photos, facts, and videos.

INDEX